The Estuary

By the same author

Poetry

LOSS OF THE MAGYAR

THE SURVIVORS

JUST LIKE THE RESURRECTION

Autobiography

MRS BEER'S HOUSE

The Estuary

Patricia Beer

MACMILLAN

© Patricia Beer 1971

First published 1971 *by*
MACMILLAN AND COMPANY LTD
London and Basingstoke
Associated Companies in New York Toronto
Dublin Melbourne Johannesburg & Madras

SBN boards: 333 12582 7
SBN paper: 333 12582 5

Printed in Great Britain by
THE BOWERING PRESS PLYMOUTH

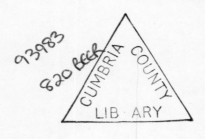

Contents

Acknowledgements

GRATEFUL acknowledgements are made to the following periodicals in which some of these poems first appeared: *Cornhill Magazine*, *The Listener*, *New Statesman*, *New York Times*, *Sunday Times*, *Twentieth Century*.

FOR JOHN AND ARNOLD

The Estuary

A light elegant wall waves down
The riverside, for tidiness
Or decoration – this water
Needs little keeping in – but turns
The corner to face the ocean
And thickens to a bastion.

No one can really taste or smell
Where the salt starts but at one point
The first building looks out to sea
And the two sides of the river
Are forced apart by cold light
And wind and different grasses.

I see this now, but at one time
I had to believe that the two
Sides were almost identical.
I was a child who dared not seem
Gloomy. Traversing grey water
From the east side where I was born

And had spent a normal cross life,
To live gratefully with strangers
On the west side, I grinned and clowned.
I did not go back for ages
And became known for cheerfulness
In a house where all was not well.

Grief was a poltergeist that would
Not materialise but broke

Everything. Neither believed in
Nor dreaded, it took one decade
To appear, one to be recognised,
Then cleared the air wonderfully

So that nowadays I am able
To see the estuary as two
Distinct pieces of countryside,
Not a great deal to choose between
Them perhaps but at least different,
Rising normally from two roots.

On one bank stiff fields of corn grow
To the hilltop, are draped over
It surrealistically.
On the other, little white boats
Sag sideways twice every day
As the sea pulls away their prop.

Looking Back

When Troilus died he was given food
And a hilltop like one more god

High enough up to hear music
Of a new kind. He could look back

On his fighting and on the plain
Where his blood still held the dust down.

Being detached now seemed a skill
He had mastered, not a windfall.

It was very easy at first
From that height to look down on lust,

Note with the cool eyes of a saint
His girl sleeping in Diomede's tent

And dwell on the futility
Of human relationships, free

As a convict in the first five
Minutes before the dogs sniff

After his escape. It was not
Long though before he saw earth start

To turn again and the saddening
Green stain of the spring widening.

Christmas Eve

The roofs over the shops
Are grey and quiet already.
In two hours from now
Light and noise will drain
From counter and cash desk
Into the streets and away.

People will go home
To windows that all year
Turned into their rooms
But goggle outwards now
With lit-up trees.

Tinsel wriggles in the heating.
Everything hangs.

As it gets dark a drunk
Comes tacking up the road
In a white macintosh
Charming as a yacht.

Dilemma

Read about the Buddhist monk.
When seven brigands move through the still trees
To murder him he yells so loud
That businessmen in Peking
Look up, twenty miles away.
We must admire him.

But what a comfort
To see the Queen in corny historical plays
Pin up her hair, thank her ladies,
Forgive everybody and go
With only a sidelong glance
At the man with the axe.

Which ought I to be?

One Man One Vote

My railwayman father voted
Only once in his entire life.
Politics was for the children
Of this present world and not for
Those who were marching to Zion.

He would not even vote Tory
Though he knew they had the breeding
And wealth that could help you, and though
The local candidate's daughter
Had by chance the same name as me.

Yet at sixty-three he went out
One evening, furtive after dark
But swashbuckling, down to the polls
To vote for a man who once worked
On the railways; a guard, Father thought.

The Branch Line

One train was the last.
Decorated with a crowd
Of people who like last things,
Not normally travellers,
Mostly children and their fathers,
It left to a theatrical blast
As the guard for once played
At his job, with mixed feelings.

Photographers were there,
For the only time perhaps
Since the railway groped
Down into these shires
First of all, and the squires
Fretted about their deer.
There were flags and a few maps,
And cheers as the signal dropped.

The platform is now old
And empty, but still shows
The act of waiting.
Beyond it the meadows,
Where once the toy shadows
Of funnel and smoke bowled,
Are pure green, and no echoes
Squeeze into the cutting.

The villages that gave
The stations their names
Were always out of sight,

Behind a hill, up a lane,
Dead, except when a train
Fetched somebody forth alive.
But now no one at all comes
Out of them by this route.

The level-crossing gates
Guard passers-by from nothing
Now. The railway's bite
Is dislocated by time,
Too out-of-date to harm
Like a gummy old cat's.
The road is the frightening
Power, the current favourite.

If the particular fast
Bright dragon of childhood
Is null, I feel the same,
Extinct; not obsolete
Nor dead, but lightweight.
The line has left no ghost
Even, but is as void
As my discarded name.

My past has been defaced
Because it ran together
So often with this line.
Trains exist elsewhere
But different, sinister:
Heads, looking out for a last
Good-bye, freeze and weather
To the sky, as at Tyburn.

The Funeral

Staring up the cold lane from the lych-gate
We swing round. The bell may have been tolling
For some time but we notice it now
Worming its way through the falling snow towards us,
A heartbeat suddenly clamouring
After years of health.

The church door is open, both sides
Hooked back, as though a mammoth
Was waddling to burial.

The tree by the church tower
Is sheltered in harbour.
The tombstones are out at sea
And would shake in the storm
If our eyes were not blunt.

The coffin is delivered
With my aunt's name on it.
She seems to be the recipient.

The wind blows texts about us as we walk
Behind the invisible body to the becalmed church.
The out-of-date middle-class voice
Of this vicar whom none of us has seen before
Scatters like torn bits of Bible:
'Am the Resurrection and'
'Worms shall destroy this'
'Flesh shall I see'.
Not really gibberish.

Death stays outside, not everywhere
As they used to tell us about God
But at the far end of the churchyard
Out of the wind, in the new grave.
We walk towards it.

But we reach nothing.

We are still three feet away from death.
Cold insteps and cold palms are not yet
Cold armpits and a cold groin.
'Blessed be the'.

Happy Ending

God guard you, storybook hero,
At risk under the sail which the wind shouts down.
The heroine on land
Sees the edge of the storm in a headache of seagulls
And is already arranging
Her eyes to look without envy
At happy half-couples
Made to be re-united.

Live through the endless rain.
Stamp on the quayside at last
With stiff boots and soft feet.
Quick, send a nosey bystander to her house
With the news, before resignation
Closes her throat.

Within a year teach her to think
That great happiness is a knack
She has learned or was born with.
Before tomorrow morning make her realise
She is not the survivor
But has a very fair chance
Of dying before you.

A Birthday Card

Best wishes for your birthday
Come with a brig in the top
Fifth of the picture, perching
On sea more tentatively
Than the muscular gulls that
Beat the air at its own game.

It is a fine day, towards
Evening. The scarlet sun rolls
Casually down the sky
Which is matt and featureless.
There is not much likelihood
Of shipwreck at the moment.

Four-fifths of the picture are
A cross-section of the sea
Reaching down farther than light.
Here sits a large mermaid. She
Is heavy, with thick bones, wide
Flesh and a tail that would crush

A drowned man's foot if it lolled
On to it. She is patient,
Too sure of herself to be
Otherwise. She combs her hair
Over her breasts which poke through,
And flexes her tail and waits.

She is charming, yellow hair,
Huge bust, a barmaid under
Water. Her red navel

Is a spot flung off the sun.
She has prospered, with bracelets
And an ornate mirror, worth

Wrecking some woman for. Just
Behind her swim two fish, grouped,
One big, one smaller, a touch
That looks both domestic and
Mythical, Adam and Eve
They seem, Mary and offspring.

This card, archetypal as
It is, could suit nobody.
Mother's boy, bitch's victim,
Henpecked husband might all be
Affronted. Everyone else
Would find it irrelevant.

The Bull

The bull on the poster speaks
Trunkless but not just a head.
Up in London to be sold
His white face that all his sons wear
Is a man's fortune.

He was once a danger.
Even across three meadows
His walk gave him away
Bred stories and giggling fright.
Without any rage he was
Thunder in a field.

Nobody except me seems
To notice him by day
But one night after the rush hour
Someone must have done,

Someone who felt the need
To draw a loop out of his mouth
Saying I AM A BULL.

Arms

I was brought up to believe
In the Everlasting Arms
And took comfort for some years
In the fatherly muscle
And grip, but fell out of them
Gradually and in slow
Motion as God dissolved. Fell
Into nightmares about arms

And specially one picture
Of the world lying flooded
With all the animals drowned,
Visible still in one foot
Of water, frozen, never
To wriggle with the tide or
Rustle to pieces. Stiff-legged
The sheep who could not embrace

And flex as the lions could
Nevertheless lay in their
Ramrod protectiveness
Holding each other like bars.
These limbs were not immortal
And, perishing, they woke me
As in a story I heard:
When my grandfather went down

With his brig in the North Sea
On a calm clear evening
There was no wireless to send

Last love on. He put his arms
Round his son and there he stood,
Protector, up to his knees
In death, and that was the last
That anyone saw of him.

The Eyes of the World

When I was a child only one hope
Enabled me to consider death:
Not heaven but the eyes of the world.
In those days it was chiefly the king
Who attracted widespread attention.
When his 'life moved peacefully
Towards its close' no one went to bed
Till dawn, music stopped, cold crowds screwed up
Their eyes at a tiny bulletin
Stuck on the railings. Some of them went
Home to sew loyal black bands on sleeves.

Something like this I felt might make it
Tolerable: if everyone would stare
At my last breaths and speak about them.
Not being a royal child I had
To shine somehow. I worked hard at it,
Turned poet for a lying-in-state
As though comfort came from cut flowers.
A long time ago this was. But still
When I see men on the moon, stepping
Into new dust with a trail of cheers
And phone calls from earth following them
I think again of the world watching

And of the subjects caught in its gaze.
For women it was nearly always
Involuntary. Leda, Mary
Were probably at peace in the hours
Before the god assumed his feathers

And swooped. Their sons with their miracles
Became as much talked of as new stars,
The minute of their making described
Everywhere, but brought them pain and were
Finally fitted into the sky.
Mankind still contemplates these women.

The martyrs Latimer and Ridley,
Who more or less chose, obviously thought
It a consolation to be watched.
Walking in the street for the last time
Past the civilised buildings they had
To leave, conversing for the last time,
One cheered the other with fantasies
Of the candle that they would become
After the flare of burning, a small
Focus but hypnotic till doomsday.
Did this help them ten minutes later?

I do not rely on watchers now,
Guessing that all we can count on from
The eyes of the world is that they spot
The trivialities we prefer
To keep dark. In death I quite expect
The audience shut their eyes before we
Shut ours, tiptoe out of the ward, turn
Off the television as the shots
Are fired. I cannot imagine now
Why I believed they were the answer.

The Underground Garage

In late evening we have come back
To the garage, and are now driving
Up and up the ramp, revving
The concrete underworld away behind us,

Where a few cars in the stale light
Are always questing among the settled
Paralysed ones. Now the bad breath
Of the garage meets the no-breath

Outside. Two months ago Hyde Park
Breathed mildly, wetly and its leaves
Fell in a twist of scents. Winter
Has made everything too dead to smell.

With twenty yards to go before
The night, our lamps' beam confronts
A column of dead leaves advancing
Down the tunnel towards us.

Dead, curled, colourless, stiff,
They march away from their trees, and spread
A sort of thin plausible life
Over the concrete. Dead, thrusting.

The Coming of the Cat

Everyone knows the black cat
Who curled up for centuries
On witches' laps, read aloud
From books of spells, was present
At sin even with back turned,
Who wore strange robes like nightgowns,
Looked cross rather than wicked.

Completely academic
To us now that we have one.
By day we love her from strong
To weak, put down food, stroke, tease,
Admire. She is sealed away
From us in an element
Without speech without fingers.

The breathing of air gives us
No common ground, nor does love
Of sun. She might as well be
Underwater, heaviness
Pumped out of her by the sea,
Or placid in fire, beyond
Our burning and our drowning.

Primitive man, I suppose,
Put her wherever she is
When he stepped from pure shadow
Into a dappled hunter's

World and murdered his siblings
As he once thought them to be.
Indoors became his retreat

Though not full sanctuary.
His women pay off old scores
To this day in some countries
Suckling puppies and kittens.
A gesture merely. The cat
Will always be far-fetched now,
An exotic by daylight.

But at night she has begun
To enter into our dreams.
She comes towards us, smoothly
Along the track of her own
Glare, one foreleg stuck out stiff
As a crutch, an aureole
Of claws around her bright foot.

She comes close and mutilates
Us. Daytime scratches and play
Are now deep wounds. We fear her
Especially when she changes.
Twice I saw her turn into
My mother. For my husband
She frequently becomes me.

Neither of us ever kept
A cat before. Middle-age
Is a tricky time for new
Experiences. We live
In town and keep the windows
Shut. We have been taught to take
Our dreaming like medicine.

Night ticks on. Here in Hampstead
No owls hoot and the church clock
In the 'village' is throttled
Till seven tomorrow morning.
Our kitten sleeps, a four-pound
Weight, round and black in darkness,
Pins down the quilt above us.

The Cat in the Tree

If I had been a tough child
And climber of trees it would
Be obvious why my stomach,
My legs and all my senses
Move with our cat as she steps
On to the bough and it bends.

When the garden first let her go
Slinging her against the trunk
And upwards I felt only
Praise of her black rocketing
But as she halts at bird height
To change course and her paws spy

Out her way along the air
Now I experience it.
I see her weight as the branch dips
But it has become mine too.
I look both up at her and
Down with her. I dread falling.

I stand here taking time off
In a torturer's heyday –
The news this morning was bad –
To go back to a simple
Necessary fear, the leaves
Panicking, the wood yielding.

The Killing of Sparrows

I see nothing of the killing of sparrows.
They are laid out on the kitchen floor,
Presents from the killer,
Or so the cat books say.

I looked long and closely at the first.
In death it was full of surprises:
Its beak huge, the only part of it
That was not already shrinking.
More grey feathers than I realised
A sparrow had. Beadiness gone
A prophetic look about its eyes.
Claws changed from movement to gesture.

Secondhand murder.
I indulge the killer.

I look more casually now.
Bigger as the cat grows, as the year goes on,
The dead birds tick and chime
The cat's life away, mine
And the strength of the town house.

First Love

He sat there one winter telling me a story.
He had come back from church, pale and beautiful,
After a requiem mass for a friend, no, for a comrade.
He was an atheist but for the widow's sake
Had held a candle. He mimed it for me.

The word comrade obviously meant war.
I asked, sensitively. Five winters earlier
When cold first crept in under the arcades
Ousting summer that had lain there so long
These two were walking in the dark streets

Men of the Resistance so no doubt making plans
When gunfire hurled one of them down dead
And the shuttered houses gave no sign at all.
It was a one-sentence story. At its close
I stepped on to the battlefield though the war was over.

Here was someone who had seen men die
By violence aimed at them, not random.
I had never met it in my impregnable childhood,
By the clock tower, in the shopping centre
Of my home town. I was the village idiot.

Up to now he and I had sung Alpine songs –
La Montanara, Sul Ponte di Bassano –
With feeling, been cynical and worldly
Each in a foreign language. He had said
How intelligent English girls were. And now this.

A few afternoons later we made love.
He was mild and ineffectual (I now know)
And afterwards apologetic which surprised me.
Then we went out to see a film about people
Shooting each other, pure Bang Bang You're Dead.

The Faithful Wife

I am away from home
A hundred miles from the blue curtains
I made at Christmas and the table
My grandfather brought back from Sorrento.
I am a career woman at a conference.
I love my husband. I value
Both what I own and what I do.

I left the forsythia half yellow,
The bluebells – lifted from a wood in Suffolk
Last year – still tight, the mint surfacing.
I must sweep the paths when I get back.

And here for the past week you and I
Have been conducting a non-affair
That could not even be called flirtation
That could not be called anything
Except unusually straightforward desire,
Adultery in the heart.
Life is so short.

The programme is ending.
11.30 – Conference disperses.
I watch everybody leaving.
It feels like grief, like the guillotine.

Your turn now; go home
With the 'Good-bye, love'
You use to every personable woman.

Get in your large car which ten years ago
Was full of sand and children's things
On summer evenings.
You are middle-aged now, as I am.
Write your notes up,
Fix the rattling window,
Keep your marriage vows. As I shall.

Group of Islands

Jigsaw of a county.
The green sea has unmade a shire

But narrowly.
Nowhere is the sea-bed
Much more than an arm's length away.
Danger is compressed
Into a few feet of ocean
And the navigator's skill
Must be sharper than his funny stories.

Through mild winters and tart summers
Earth and water keep in close touch.
A dog barks at a shag
That holds its breast as high
As an Egyptian cat.
A gob of foam hops into the boat.

People intermarry.
After a traumatic voyage
You see the same faces.
And the wind at its worst
Pierces everybody and strings them together.

Just beyond the last reef,
Where puffins can be spotted in lucky weather,
Down go the rocks without trace, down,
Too deep now to be called submerged,
Into a darkness where no comparisons are possible
Miles below the fields
That raise flowers like tissue paper
And gorse like lions.

Fish Pond in Lisbon

Level and weightless and still
They lie in water. The hot
Leaves of the waterlilies
Overlap in scales and look
Much more like fish than they do.

The flick of water-boatmen
Out in the air twelve inches
Above them looks like motion
As we know it, but the red
Fish lunge forward out of shade

Like a bright idea and seem
Not an act but the mind laid
Bare. They knock against the skin
Of the fish-pond from inside
With the movement of a blush

And while we lean arguing
Over the picturesque bridge
Our mirrored heads are only
Talking points in the red swirl
That cannot reach conclusion.

In Memory of Constance Markiewicz

The kind of woman that men poets
Hope their own and their friends' daughters
Will not resemble, a rarity.

Stepping from silk into uniform,
From earth to dirt, she lit out and left
The green county where her father ruled

Then left her husband and child also
Like an evangelist with a wilder
Calling or a painter feeling trapped.

Women do not usually do this.
She calls to mind Mrs Jellyby
That pretty monster who looked over

Her children's heads into Africa
Though she would not have died, I suppose,
For the good of Boorioboola.

Constance felt the value of bloodshed
As deeply as Pearse and Connolly.
She bespoke a priest to see her through

The bullets, but did not require him
For eleven years and then bloodlessly,
Having gone far past disappointment.

Yes, she became opinionated
And shrill, but had a longer funeral
Procession than most of us will have.

Picture of Workers Resting

You lie cooling and sleeping, the heat
Just round the corner of the haystack
And the work spread out over the field.

Your two billhooks put tidily down
And each pair of shoes taken off look
Much more like a couple than you do

Though man and wife you lie side by side
Apparently trusting each other.
Rest from work seems no real bond at all.

How very old-fashioned it all is.
The cart now stands in a museum
Of ancient crafts, the clothes have rotted.

A Marxist critic says the painter
Understood perfectly your bowed heads
And degradation. Perhaps he did,

But more profoundly, as creator
Not critic, saw his own flesh and blood
Lying there and did not ask himself

If you would have been quick at learning
To read, given the chance, or worthy
Landowners, given a piece of land.

Self-help

I was brought up on notions of self-help,
Not that it was so-called and none of us
Had read or heard of Samuel Smiles; perhaps
Fortunately, as his pioneers,
Artists and inventors were all men.
Women could be useful or obstructive,
Hungry, in tears, or steadfast like the wife
Of Flaxman, but they had to play the game
Of Help the Genius till their dying day.

I looked down on ne'er-do-wells and wastrels,
Did homework all the evening, winter and summer,
Took the Scholarship, School Cert and Higher.
It was the only way to rise above
Being a maid or serving in a shop.
All this went with religion very well,
The Christian message seeming to be that if
You didn't help yourself in worldly matters
Nobody else was at all likely to.

It worked, and now I sit in Hampstead Village
On a Georgian sofa reading Samuel Smiles
In paperback with afterword and foreword.
Makers of stocking-frames and bobbin-net
Machines, discoverers of vaccination,
New techniques in surgery and how
To classify the strata of the earth,
Watch late into the fireless night, get up
To foggy dawns, gag at poor food, and strive.

But not together. Each striver is alone.
If by accident they help each other
Or their paths cross it seems quite out of keeping:
As when Scott, the former copying clerk,
Offers a lift – outside, of course – to Kemp
The shepherd's son who was to build the Scott
Memorial. There is no pattern in it.
The individual is on his own
With his furnace or his telescope.

Self-help is dangerous. In the tall half-light
Of the cathedral Galileo could
Have counted years of peril in the swinging
Lamp. Böttger is buried like a dog
At night. And many of the heroes have
The Luddites to contend with. See them standing
Piebald in torchlight, flames and shouts behind them
As their inventions come to grief. Sometimes
Their daughters have to scuttle into pawnshops.

Here I sit reading, intermittently conscious
Of the people in the alley – Cockney
Accents threatening to a countrywoman
Even after all these years – returning
From the wash-house to their bathless flats
In Peabody-type buildings, and of the problem
Children smashing up someone's milk bottles,
Getting nearer. They live now. Unlike
The resolute contenders of my book,

Unlike my father and my grandfather
Who worked so hard and never helped themselves,
And unlike me in another sense who might
Have come straight out of *Self-help* on my worst days,
Practising lawful self-advancement, preaching

It, enjoying its rewards. And through
The white comfortable mist a wind blows holes
Lays bare the quagmire reaching for us all
Whispers how soon we could be shouting 'Help'.

Victorian Trains

I MR DOMBEY

The whistle blows. The train moves.
Thank God I am pulling away from the conversation
I had on the platform through the hissing of steam
With that man who dares to wear crape for the death of my son.
But I forget. He is coming with us.
He is always ahead of us stoking the engine.
I depend on him to convey me
With my food and my drink and my wraps and my reading
    material
To my first holiday since grief mastered me.
He is the one with the view in front of him
The ash in his whiskers, the speed in his hair.

He is richer now. He refused my tip.
Death and money roll round and round
In my head with the wheels.
I know what a skeleton looks like.
I never think of my dead son
In this connection. I think of wealth.
The railway is like a skeleton,
Alive in a prosperous body,
Reaching up to grasp Yorkshire and Lancashire
Kicking Devon and Kent
Squatting on London.
A diagram of growth
A midwinter leaf.

I am a merchant
With fantasies like all merchants.
Gold, carpets, handsome women come to me

Out of the sea, along these tracks.
I am as rich as England,
As solid as a town hall.

II LADY GLYDE

The gardener is bringing the elegant luggage
Someone got for me as a bride.
I have never ordered anything for myself.
He approaches along the country platform
To receive the present for his children.
The housekeeper has been buying my ticket.
How I wish you were coming with me
Faithful housekeeper. I am going to my death
Away from my unhappy home.
You are self-righteous and less wealthy than I am.
I could rely on you now as though I were very ill.

This track is no way of escape for me.
My enemy, my husband's friend,
Will meet me at the terminus.
Though I run through the sewers of the city for days
Till at last I see round light at the end
The outlet will be barred by a grid.
I am man-handled.

I look down from the carriage window.
I am the fields and the houses
That the railway pushed aside.
The whistle blows. The train moves.

Safe Lives

This actor with the cow-brown sweater stands
Theatrically still. The Albert Hall
Is half-way through an Evening of Free Greek
Music and Drama. We have had a choir,
An orchestra, songs and a guitar,
And now have come to Aristophanes,
Euripides, the Students' Trial, the Edict
On Censorship. Nobody in the audience
Disagrees. It is all very peaceful.

He speaks, beautifully, and dominates.
Last week we saw him naked in a film.
He is Philoctetes, beseeching those
Who come across him with his running wound
And leave him, to show some humanity.
Pleading does not move them so he threatens:
Open your safe lives to the grief of others.
Disaster strikes down the secure. A strange
Remark. Disaster strikes down anybody.

We have good seats, he seems to look at me.
But I am not secure. I have not gone
Mad yet, neither am I very good
At screaming – I should like to be – but I
Am not secure. And no doubt those who heard
Philoctetes raged dumbly back at him
Throttled with terrors as they stood calmly,
Cheerfully even, by the summer sea.

Ezra Pound Leaves Rome

Morning in the city fills empty
Streets wall to wall. The cars have fled north
With frightened politicians in them.
No citizens with handcarts of home
Follow. Those guns are liberators.

Everyone is indoors. If your bell
Fearfully rings it is the 'traitor'
Who has made no plans for this event
Asking you for boots and a road map
Things he has not needed since boyhood.

Which is the road north in a modern
City? How can he find where it starts?
To leave a city on foot is forced
Especially carrying a knapsack
With bread and tea, and a walking stick.

He has been living for a long time
In a world of his own, but now he
Steps into the landscape, heading north,
Almost studying the position
Of the sun, the length of the shadows.

Autobiography

I sailed through many waters,
Cold following warm because I moved
Though Arctic and equator were steady.

Harbours sank as I discarded them,
Landmarks melted into the sky
When I needed them no longer.

I left behind all weathers.
I passed dolphins, flying-fish and seagulls
That are ships in their own stories.